ARTISTS AT WAR

DRAWN IN BA

Sketches of the 51st Highland Division from El Alamein until the defeat of Rommel and the Afrika Korps.

A haircut, desert style, during a lull. North Africa, late 1942.

Dedicated to the men of the Highland Division who fought and died that freedom might live.

INTRODUCTION

The Battle of El Alamein began on the night of the 23rd October 1942 when 882 field and medium guns, opening fire simultaneously, unleashed a ferocious barrage upon the German and Italian lines. Darkness became daylight, and the noise was deafening. Such was the start of the biggest, and most famous, Allied attack of the North African campaign in the Second World War. From this moment onwards, the upsets, defeats and setbacks of the desert war so far were forgotten and the advance to victory began. The incredible series of sketches within this book, some in colour and some black and white, help illustrate the part that the men of the 51st Highland Division played in this almost never ending march westwards. They are a vivid and contemporary insight into the lives of the ordinary soldiers living and fighting in this highly mobile desert war. Indeed, few histories of the North African Campaign are capable of

providing such a stark image of the conditions and deprivations they were forced to endure as Aston Fuller does with his sketches and captions, which were completed at the time and on the spot!

Aston Fuller was born in Swansea, South Wales, on the 25th February 1906, and was a student at the Grammar School, and later at the Swansea School of Arts & Crafts. After a period in America, he returned to Swansea to set up a studio that dealt mainly in commercial art, before taking up the post of Display Manager with the George Hopkinson Organisation. Fuller was called up for military service in October 1940. In 1942, as a member of the Royal Artillery (R.A.), he was posted to the 51st Highland Division in North Africa. In 1943 he was attached to the Headquarters R.A. of the 51st Highland Division as a

Signaller. From there he became a L/Bdr. in 490/126 Field Regt. R.A., of the Mediterranean Expeditionary Force, before serving in the 51st (H) Anti-Tank Regt. R.A. Whilst a Signaller, Fuller was Mentioned in Despatches for Distinguished Service - repairing a broken signals line under enemy fire. Having fought across North Africa, the Highland Division, and Fuller, returned to Europe to participate in the D-Day operations before ending the war in Holland. Fuller was 'demobbed' in October 1945, only to speak very rarely about his war service. He sadly died, quite suddenly, in March 1959 at the comparatively early age of 53.

On his posting to North Africa, Fuller had taken with him three small sketch books, a supply of coloured crayons and some carbons and pencils, and succeeded in completing well over 50 sketches depicting the events that unfolded around him. Not being an accredited War Artist, he still had to contribute to the combat, completing many of these sketches from the relative safety of a foxhole or slit trench in the forward areas.

On Aston Fuller's return home on leave in 1944, a publisher was found to produce the sketches in book form as a memorial to the men and achievements of the 51st Highland Division. When preparations were well advanced, an application was made to the Ministry of Information for release of the necessary paper allocation, in view of the stringent wartime rationing. This was refused and, sadly, the project was abandoned. So here, for the first time since the book was created nearly 60 years ago, is the almost complete series of sketches by Aston Fuller, providing a unique and contemporary depiction of the victory in North Africa.

1: 'Tommies bathing in the Mediterranean'

Before El Alamein; October 1942.

The bathing parade was one of the British 'Tommy's' desert joys. The first intimate contact with the blue Mediterranean Sea and the opportunity to cleanse himself of the desert dust - a swim in the clear water.

War is forgotten for a few hours, for too soon would come the night and with it the hard, gruelling 'digging in'. The guns of Montgomery's Army would soon be brought up and the pits dug.

Upon the shelving beach one would gaze westward along the coastline, the eye roving towards the enemy lines - Rommel, perhaps, relaxing in the sun! Great days were these - and greater the expectations! Setbacks had been ours, but now sun-tanned bodies held a fresh hope. The most glorious page in the British Army's history was near.

In moments of quiet, Aston Fuller would often sketch portraits of those men and officers with whom he served - often at their request. Here is just one example - Bombardier Flett. There will, no doubt, be other survivors of the Desert War who still cherish a portrait of themselves that was completed in the field by Aston Fuller.

Bombardier Flett.

PLEASE READ INSTRUCTIONS BEFORE USE
PLEASE RETAIN INSTRUCTIONS FOR FUTURE REFERENCE
FM RADIO ALARM CLOCK

Features:
1: Speakers
2: Radio Volume & ON/OFF
3: Alarm ON/OFF
4: Scan Radio
5: Reset Radio
6: Alarm Set
7: Time Set
8: Hour
9: Minute

FM scan range 88-108 Mhz

BATTERY INSTALLATION remove the battery compartment cover at the back of the unit, insert 3 * AA/1.5V batteries (batteries not supplied) into the battery compartment ensuring correct polarity is observed then replace the compartment cover.

OPERATION-

TO OPERATE THE RADIO-Slide the ON/OFF dial at the top of the radio unit to the left.
- Press the SCAN button until a radio station is found. Keep pressing the scan button until you have found the desired FM radio station.
- To adjust the volume, slide the ON/OFF dial at the top of the radio unit to the right for more volume and to the left for less volume.
- To turn off the radio, slide the ON/OFF dial at the top of the radio unit to the far left until you hear a click.

To improve the radio signal fully extend the antenna.

TO SET THE TIME - Turn off the radio function.
- Press down on the TIME button, whilst pressing the TIME button, press down simultaneously on the MIN Button to set the minutes and the HOUR button to set the hour.

TO SET THE BUZZER ALARM -Press down the ARM button. Whilst pressing the ARM button, press down simultaneously on the "HOUR" button to set the hour and press down simultaneously on the "MIN" button to set the minute.

To check the alarm set time when the display is showing time, press ARM button.

To turn the alarm ON/OFF press the ALARM button.

WARNING-
- Do not dispose of batteries in fire.
- Never use old and new batteries together.
- Do not use different types of battery together.
- Batteries must be inserted following the correct polarity shown on the unit.
- Remove exhausted batteries from the unit and dispose of safely.
- Remove batteries if unit is not in use for a long time.
- Do not expose the unit to rain, moisture or extreme temperatures.
- Do not place near strong magnets.

This appliance conforms to EC Directive 2004/108/EC with respect to Electromagnetic Compatibility and ROHS directive 2002/95/EC

Made in China

2: 'Repairing the line of communication - Forward Observation Post'   El Alamein; October 1942.

The last ridge held by the Germans was taken. The Scots named it "The Nairn". It had to be held - it <u>was</u> held! The 'eyes of the guns' were able to over-look the enemy positions. Signallers working under heavy fire to keep the line of communications open - exposure meant instant death!

Only by night could the OP be entered or vacated, and to repair the 'break' - which happened on the last 70 yards of wire - entailed a slow, crawling process. Now and again a few shells would fall uncomfortably close. The tense moments wondering whether the next bore your name! Mending hurriedly, crawling, and clutching sandy rubble to reach the post, and still lying low. Throwing a pebble at the stone-protected OP - surprised voices answering "line is OK." A hurried backing away, reaching half way over the ridge - then a low stumbling run to the rear OP - the job accomplished! The OP keeps its eyes on the enemy!

3: 'A near miss'   E Troop, 126 Field Regt. R.A. Battle of El Alamein; November 1942.

Sudden death all around! The guns were temporarily silent - the Germans had located our position. High in the sky the tell tale burst of his airburst ranging shells - the quick order "get under cover"!

Near the Command Post an un-exploded shell furrowed and screeched along the gravel-like sand finally coming to a halt, a spent, lifeless object - thank God! Behind the post, in slit trenches, lay the inert figures of men off-duty.

A few minutes previously one of the 'Tommies' mentally debated which trench to use - his own or the next. He chose the next - it was deeper. The whining sound of a shell - and crunch - a vivid, orange-red flame and flying shrapnel. He was safe, but his own, vacant, trench smashed and scattered! This was the last attempt to put the guns out of action, for later Rommel pulled out from El Alamein. The greatest advance in history had begun.

4

4: 'Early morning wash and shave'   November 1942.

A lack of water was not allowed to interfere with the usual morning ablutions. Many times the pint mug, the daily ration, was the only means of ensuring personal cleanliness. The rest of the day would be hot and dusty - there would be no opportunity for a hasty 'toilet' during the next 24 hours.

Old petrol tins cut in half, perhaps the odour of spirits still emanating, would come in useful. Sand dust gradually darkens the already murky water. Someone, his own meagre supply upset, dashes up for a shave.... good-humoured banter and chiding from his mate! Ingenuity in lighting a fire was a gift that the desert soldier quickly acquired. The fire appeared from nowhere - his shaving water in a castaway potato tin perched precariously over the flame. From Commander to ordinary ranker, the desert was no respecter of persons - they all marched without water!

5

6

5: 'The dust storm'
November 1942.

The Brigade rests after the strenuous battle to replenish and bring up stores. Kit to be cleaned - bivouacs erected in scattered layout - guns camouflaged. Late afternoon - towards dinner-time - the day heavy and sultry - there is no life in the air - the sky appears too blue!
The guard clean their rifles and scrubbed white kit - the rank and file troop to Dinner. To the south-west, across the distant horizon - a low, dark mass - gaining in dimension - its colour, brown - our first dust storm! The guard about to mount. Tents hurriedly pegged down are made firmer. Everyone vanishes, for the storm is upon us!
Through the canvas flaps the sand works its way - heads are buried under clothes - nostrils are filled with grit and breathing becomes harder. Sleep is no way of escape. The wind tears and howls across the miles of desert. Hours pass - no abatement! Then early morning - and silence! The dust storm has passed on.

6: 'The lonely Cairn'
After El Alamein; November 1942.

Tribute, then, to the Battalion of Black Watch whose assault on the "Nairn" ridge - the last vantage-point of the enemy - was crowned with victory. The cross-topped cairn, built in hasty reverence, contained the hallowed dead. The cross resolutely buried deep among the stones - its rough-hewn arms a challenge.
Around were marked the tracks of armoured vehicles. The steel helmet, shrapnel-torn, lay with its strap unbuckled. Across the way a half-written letter - from a soldier to his sweetheart - the ink already bleached in the sun. Half-buried bayonet; a knapsack with its 'Woodbine' cigarettes and personal kit - reminders of a supreme sacrifice!

7: 'Italian dugout on the coast road'
El Daba, Egypt; 12th November 1942.

The enemy flees before the relentless pressure of the 'Eighth'. Behind him he leaves his supplies - and the booty is large. Humour is not lacking in the grim scene. To the left, a 3-ton truck travelling at speed whilst behind, like a recalcitrant child, an Italian light field gun, bumping high off the ground its tiny wheels whirling in the air. Masses of tired and dejected prisoners - a dusty, straggling, un-military spectacle, many dazed from the terrific onslaught.
Overlooking the coast road the rocky terrain is honeycombed with deep dug shelters. Scattered over the ground endless correspondence, thousands of cards and letters - mail uncensored - and a card or two illustrating the Axis emblems casting their shadow over the Pyramids of Egypt. The depths of the dugouts bore evidence of a hurried departure. Bottles of wine, clothing and even personal belongings left behind. Cigarettes in plenty! The 'Tommy' filled his pockets. He smoked again! Down on the rock-bound shore a German mobile anti-aircraft gun, its chassis turned over, a symbol of defeat.

7

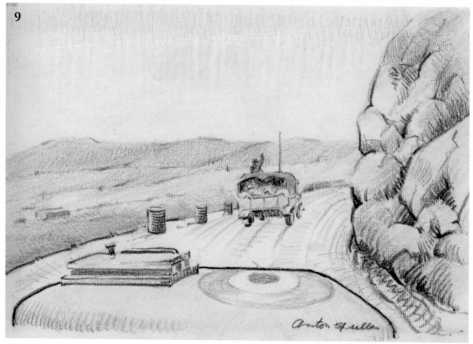

8: 'A convoy travels over the crest'   Halfaya Pass; 25th November 1942.

Perhaps the most famous Pass in the history of the desert campaign. The retreat of Rommel had produced the quickening pace of an avenging army. Here, halting on the coast road, the view of the famous Pass in the evening light made an imposing spectacle. The tiny specks of vehicles and guns, silhouetted against the golden escarpment, stand out vividly in one's memory. A halt to allow the forward elements to negotiate the Sollum Pass, as the traffic this time was dense. Eagerness to close with the enemy being the watchword of all.

An hour in which to while away the time. Vehicles and guns drawn to the side of the road; brew cans filled; fires lit; and groups of soldiers with tin mugs in hand. Satisfaction expressed only when the brew was between thirsty lips. An order to wait till dawn as the traffic was too dense - the Sollum Pass too difficult at night. Bedding-down - blankets hurriedly pulled over tired limbs. Dawn comes, the convoy moves forward.

9: 'The road over the escarpment'   Sollum Pass; 26th November 1942.

Early morning finds the vehicles and guns on the move, slowly making their way to the foot of this remarkable escarpment. The rising sun begins to cast its rays upon the sand-red mass, the crevices starting to form deep mauve shadows.

Nestling beneath lay the scarred remains of Sollum itself. The walls and dwellings are chalked and scribbled over with Axis-inspired slogans. Inside one of the smashed houses can be seen drawings of voluptuous women as well as caricatures of Allied leaders... all the one-time scene of a hectic occupation.

There is an awe-inspiring view as the convoy makes its way, slowly climbing. The Pass in places is precariously narrow - not helped by a bomb-torn hole in the hard rock below. A sheer drop of hundreds of feet - reaching the top brings a sigh of relief! The view below a shining golden panorama - the blue sea contrasting the whole.

10

10: 'The water truck'   27th November 1942.

The most treasured possession in the desert. The enemy's greatest delight was to try and 'strafe' the most valuable vehicle - the water truck. In his many sorties along the coast road this was one of his main targets. Indeed, the loss of this vehicle could place a whole Battery in a very awkward position!

The reliance upon a stringent water economy was mainly responsible for the successful continuance of a water supply. The one driver in the unit possessed of great patience is the 'Waterman', his task not made easier by the thirsty soldier who endeavours to coax an extra ration. He had a long journey to a watering-point left far behind - then bringing his precious supply to the front line. To replenish a gun group meant that only one person took the cans - the risk too great to allow a queue.

11

12

11: 'Cleaning the guns'
November 1942.

After a long journey, the long lines of guns and vehicles slowly come to a stop. The Command to 'bed-down' for the night. Dawn - and the word is to rest for some days.

The sojourn is welcome. Now can the hundred and one matters of adjustment be made regarding the smooth running of trucks, and the all-important task of cleaning the guns. Under the camouflage nets the Gunners toil in the sun. Desert dust - the cruel enemy of smooth mechanism - is removed. The numerous parts of kit laid out for inspection. The frenzied racking of brains to endeavour to trace a lost tool or bolt. Then the sun sets in the west and the Gunner rests. His eyes look northwest - he thinks of home!

12: 'The Ward Orderly at the Field Hospital'
Agedabia, 15th December 1942.

The first glimpse of the Field Hospital was a source of great relief. To those with minor ailments it meant a few days of respite - a short, but more than welcome, break from front-line duties. To those less fortunate, the skill of the surgeon was of paramount, if not greater, importance.

Various tented wards would be set up. In the centre a large Red Cross would be displayed over the ground. Admittance to the Field Hospital might, perhaps, be the result of lying in a filthy enemy dug slit trench - the uncomfortable experience of skin irritation - and now a complete cleansing. Quick friendships; exchange of yarns; of near escapes, and always the photographs from home. The Ward Orderly, with his good humour and patience, proving a valuable aid to a quick recovery.

13: 'Patients playing cards at the Field Hospital'
Agedabia, 16th December 1942.

Night comes. To while away the time was the patient's problem. A pack of cards was his solution. Between the rows of reclining figures an emergency case would be brought in. A respectful silence - a chum perhaps. Who knew?

The flickering oil lamp casting its faded light to no great distance - the players straining to see their 'hands'. A soldier's low chuckle over someone's quick rejoinder. Others turning over to begin the long night's sleep. Outside - darkness. The drone of an enemy plane. The muffled sound of exploding bombs. Men sitting up, straining every nerve. Comments on the raid - where would it be? Some heard the sound over here - some over there. Imagination flaring up. Was Rommel going to attack? Were we going in? "Lights out'."

13

14

15

14: 'Greenery and sand - the supply lines'   Agedabia, 17th December 1942.
The return to one's unit from Hospital entailed a most difficult journey because of the quick advance of the Army's front-line troops. One of the 'Good Samaritans' in the field was the vehicle taking up supplies. A chance phone-call to the nearby Supply Depot might prove an advantage. Perhaps there would be a truck the following day heading to the unit.
A spirit of comradeship - a willing co-operation - was the keynote of the Corps. Spread over the desert, the supply trucks would be scattered, each one to its allotted space. Here the desert began to show a green face. No longer a drab, brown, wind-blown expanse. Green - a welcome sight to desert sore eyes. Then moving off - back to the guns.

15: 'The Bren Gun specialist'   El Agheila, 20th December 1942.
The sun bright in the heavens, the ground sodden after heavy rains. The ridge on the left forms a natural watershed. Tumbling over rocky boulders and through deep crevices the water appears a refreshing sight. Men hastily discard garments to bathe in the rushing stream.
Rifles and Bren Guns are cleaned of any semblance of rust, for dampness can find a way under the finest of coverings.

16: 'Convoy halts near Serte'   Tripolitania, January 1943.
In desert formation the vehicles move continually forward, the sun slowly rising in the heavens. The chill of early morning turns to a warm temperature, and by midday the desert heat becomes oppressive. Viewing the long columns, stretching out in perspective, cannot be readily forgotten.
Moments of excitement as high-flying enemy aircraft endeavour to bomb the ever-advancing hordes. When the midday halt is called, the anti-aircraft guns are immediately placed in readiness for instant action. To shield themselves from the sun, the soldiers eat their light lunch on the lowered tall-boards. Some crawl under vehicles to keep cool. Meals finished, they gather in groups. The conversation turns to sport.... the family....

17

18

17: 'Brew-up tea to keep out the cold'   Near Serte, Tripolitania, 8th January 1943.

This time of year the early hours of the morning proved extremely cold. At night the temperature would fall, the cold intense. Men huddled together for warmth. Friends had sent many types of 'woollies' for the men's comfort. Scarves, balaclavas, mittens and gloves. Inside many were the addresses of the donors. A mad scramble to get one's share of the good fortune. The pleased expressions of the lucky ones, the less fortunate content with mittens'.

Around the hastily lit fire the soldiers would collect for their morning brew. Old petrol tins used as stools. A greatly enjoyed respite, and a welcome call - 'brew-up'.

18: 'Low level attack from the air'   Wadi Zemzem, January 1943.

Bivouacs just erected - the campsite between coast road and sea. The sun setting in the west.... all is tinged with a red-gold hue. The cooks down in the hollowed-out cookhouse.... driver's last-minute overhaul.... the Bren Gun placed ready in a former Italian gun pit.

General thought is comfort for the night soon to come.... but peace is not to be! Flying low over the sea race in the Axis planes. We watch their flight with more than casual interest. 'What is he up to now?' The query is quickly answered.... the rattle of cannon and ack-ack fire ever coming nearer.... the sudden excitement.... the order.... "under cover". The nearest shelter to hand - a half-dug hole in a mound. Two inert forms.... set teeth.... here it comes.... the spitting hail of bullets from the plane's guns. 'Follow my leader' they come.... a hit! Smoke appears nearby.... no one hurt, thank God!

19: 'Breakfast interlude'   Wadi Zemzem, Tuesday 12th January 1943.

Up early in the morning, the blue Mediterranean forming a background of calm. Dug in the side of the sand-earth, the slit trenches, the ever-comforting protectors, are tidied up. Blankets are folded and kit straightened. Ablutions completed. The 'staggered' march to breakfast - six men at a time for wariness is the watchword.

Breakfast over - a stroll to the rock-strewn beach to cleanse the utensils. The stillness of the morning is suddenly broken by the purr of a distant plane. Then a dozen enemy planes streak in.... a short space of time.... a few streak out again! The Spitfires anticipated their move and in they went. Close to shore the dark hull of an escaping craft.... the avenger fires a burst.... a small glow begins below the fuselage.... a desperate attempt to get away. A final burst then, hovering for a second, the Axis plane, enveloped in flames, plunges to the depths.

20

21

16

20: 'Caught unawares'   Near Misurata, Thursday 14th January 1943.

Here and there in the arid expanse, fertile ground would yield welcome 'cover'. Through the low bush and windswept trees the now-dispersed vehicles would endeavour to conceal themselves from the air. On higher ground the low-built stonework of an ancient well - already a long cord, with canvas bucket, lowered into the depths.

Groups of men wandering further away to explore a more safe and concealed place for 'bedding down'. The sun begins to set. Suddenly the sky appears pregnant with flying death. No time to look around..... one dives ground-wards and crawls beneath an overhanging bank of earth.... the gripping of loose rubble in one's hands.... gritting of teeth as the sound of steel strikes the Wadi! They are gone! The raising of many heads.... figures slowly pick themselves up.... remarks of relief. Has anybody got a cigarette? Phew....!

21: 'First glimpse of Italian settlements'   Approaching Zlitten, Tripolitania, January 1943.

Misurata falls! Now an eager move forward to cut across the desert and by-pass the coast road. Long days of travel. No rest, but a steady, relentless pursuit! Gradually the earth becomes cultivated. In the distance small white block-like objects - farmsteads. The far distant sand-hills of the Mediterranean shore appear as a mauve-hued barrier.

Stop for a few minutes.... borrowed binoculars passed around.... eagerness to view the landscape. Set out in even formation - the colonial farms - the nearby cultivation protected from the rolling sands by straight lines of desert grass. A fight for existence.... a hard living. Silence over the whole scene.... no sign of any living thing. Closer to the habitations and still no sign of life. A dog barks in the distance. Farm upon farm is passed by.... no suggestion of welcome.... they had left their farms, these people of the soil, for we were the enemy! Vicious propaganda had persuaded the colonists to flee.

22

22: 'Resting after battle'   5 miles west of Homs, 23rd January 1943.

[Homs has fallen, and the enemy left. Our tanks had thundered through chasing the enemy. Always this relentless pursuit.]

The pleasant countryside brings memories of home - greenery in its richness - small uplands and lowlands. The distant hillside is dotted with low square dwellings - the homes of the natives. Alongside the road, lying on its side, is a captured heavy mobile gun - the last definite pugnacious sign of a retreating enemy!

Tired troops, eager for a rest, line the road. Wagons pull out, others remain. Two knocked-out tanks are a grim reminder of the price of urgent close-quarter fighting. Across in the distance a castle-like building, its walls silhouetted against the skyline. A begging native.... a little food.... a conversation. By signs he acquaints us with the story of the Castle. Crossing his hands he gives the impression of chains. We grasp his meaning. British prisoners were once within those thick walls to be ultimately shipped from Homs to Italy or elsewhere! Other natives gather around for food, their pinched faces a sure sign of great privations. The British soldier, ever generous, gives what he can.

23: 'Jocks clear the road to Tripoli after Axis demolition'   24th January 1943.

At long last the goal of the Eighth Army.... Tripoli.... the jewel of Mussolini's Empire not many miles away! The enemy, with Teuton thoroughness, blows up the part of the highway that is normally a tortuous journey. The road blocked.... convoys at a standstill.... sweating, labouring men with pick and shovel clear the debris. To the right - a few native figures - strangely contrasting the whole scene - pick their way over the crest.

Suspicious thoughts.... the surmise correct.... the little band brought to a halt by Military Police. The loaded mules stand motionless as unwilling hands unloosen the binding thongs. From among the assorted loot, the familiar sight of a British firearm.... a leather belt.... the tell-tale evidence of a pilfered body. They pass below us - these unkempt scavengers of the desert! Hours pass and - as horses champing at the bit - the engines of war begin their final advance!

24: 'Flotsam and jetsam'   Tripoli Harbour, 30th January 1943.

"TRIPOLI IS OURS". These magic words are passed from mouth to mouth. This great city, little damaged by the ravages of war, presents itself - a welcome relief. The longed-for rest from continual movement. Tired troops already washing their dust-covered clothes, and bodies bathed and refreshed. Eager for sightseeing.... the native bazaars.... shopping in a once fashionable Boulevard.

The harbour-front presents a remarkable sight. A number of ships battered and sunk, and one or two wrecked at the mole entrance in a last-minute German effort to make the port useless for some time. Ugly, dark, burnt-out wharves where a large liner dominates, its hull rent open, a silent, broken thing. Italian residents begin to show themselves and walk around the waterfront. Youngsters sell sour oranges till authority spoils their efforts at victimisation. In the distance the twin pillars of stone, one topped by the symbol of Romulus, the other by a galleon. The lazing swell at the water's edge. Flotsam and Jetsam - war's aftermath'.

25: 'A humble abode in an orange grove'   Tripoli, 31st January 1943.

A dust-covered army, the glory of victory now upon their brow, the 'Tommies' erect their weather-torn bivouacs. Pleasant surroundings.... green orange-groves. Strict orders against looting.... pleasant bargaining.... then a standard price. Slowly the farms return to normal - native labourers resume their work - the huge windmills begin to turn in the freshening breeze - water is now beginning to flow.

Night falls. The sound of aircraft. Ack-ack covers the sky. Tripoli is raided. The low hiss of a falling shell.... the thud not far from the nearest tent.... excitement for a moment.... undercover against shrapnel.... then silence! The last of the raiders has gone. Under the weather-worn tent flaps blankets are rolled out. The starry sky appears between the improvised canvas covering. The 'Tommies' hoped it would not rain - but it did!

26: 'Churchill inspects the 51st'   Tripoli, February 1943.

Bustle in the camp. The guns are stripped.... the brasses are polished.... paint is found. There is to be an inspection. By whom.... when.... and why? The questions - the answers - all of varying opinions. This will definitely be a big review - and the whole thing is so hush-hush.

In the sweltering sun the guns are lined in rows.... a detailed inspection more thorough than before. Gun squads lined up.... individual checking.... helmets to boots glistening.... for isn't this a great occasion? At early dawn the guns move from their places on the Promenade. The Highland Division is on parade. The kilted pipers, figures erect, lead. The gallant men march with pride.... gone now is the dust and sweat.... the Division is proud. Towards the be-flagged stand, neath the ancient ramparts of the castle, they march. A blue-clad figure takes the salute. Winston Churchill.... God Bless Him!

27: 'The Divisional concert party'   Tripoli, 8th February 1943.

The 'Balmorals' perform at the Miramare Theatre in Tripoli.

28: 'Through a shattered window - the first convoy'   Tripoli Harbour, 9th February 1943.

An endeavour is made to bring business back to normal. Shops are now beginning to open. There is more to buy. The earlier bargains are gone - Police check on unscrupulous traders. The square of the Piazza Costello is the scene of the Changing of the Guard. The kilted pipers.... the ever absorbed interest of the inhabitants in the ceremonial! The motley crowd pressing against the barriers - the most cosmopolitan yet seen!

Nearby the unloading of ships, for now the harbour is in use again. The Royal Navy is 'on the job'. From the top of the city's largest theatre could be seen the whole expanse of the docks, and one of the shattered windows framed a busy scene. A precarious climb up to the dome-like roof, over blast-shaken brickwork, to view the city beneath. The sea is blue. There is a hum of activity. The scene melts in a distant mist.... the picture is broken.... a loud report.... guns flash. A reconnaissance plane!

29

30

29: 'The first halt in Tunisia'   Ben Gardane, 20th February 1943.
The welcome rest in Tripoli proved a stimulus to far greater efforts in the last phase of the North African campaign. The Highland Division presses onward! Through the shattered border outpost that marks the entrance into Tunisia the convoys race. The first halt and midday rest.... the sun high in the heavens.... tailboards lowered.... tea cans on the brew.... rations shared.

Personal reflection on the surroundings.... there is not much change of scene.... except upon the nearby buildings - evidence of French occupation. Conversation turns on the subject of the Mareth Line.... how far is it? The question is soon answered by the Command. 'Get ready to move off'. 'Get mounted'. We are away!

30: 'Gun positions before the Mareth Line'   Wadi Zigzaou, 28th February 1943.
Rommel prepares to show fight! The famous Mareth Line - the barrier! It afforded temporary protection against the much-vaunted Desert Army. Here in the deep Wadi must be dug the gun-pits. The large high face of the Wadi-side afforded protection for the numerous vehicles. A position has been chosen. The evening fast draws to its close.... the excellent cover of night. Command Post to be dug.... implements brought out.... every available man digging into the side of a soft earthed mound. By relays the team works far into the night.... the important task finished.

One of the most difficult of all desert experiences.... locating personal kit. The desert around - silent and friendless. Guided by noises.... low talk.... enquiries.... at last, the bedding. Groups of men 'bed-down' for the night. The last ritual.... the digging of a slit-trench. Beneath warm blankets - a canopy of stars above - at last, before Mareth, deep slumber!

31

31: 'Officers asleep at night in the Command Post'   Mareth Line, 5th March 1943.
In the side of the Wadi, excellent protection has been found. The Command Post is dug. Signallers nearby dig fresh trenches in the soft earth, some completely boxed-in on three sides, the top covered by old canvas. Great care is taken in the dispersal of trenches dug in on the gradual slope above the guns.

Across on the other side, the cookhouse is buried deep into the rocky side. A large boulder jams the entrance - a natural protection against flying shrapnel. Night falls.... duties are allotted. The Command Post - its lighted interior a most comforting sight. A large canvas cover hangs over the entrance.... the concealment of light is of paramount importance. Midnight is near.... changing of the Signaller on duty. On the position, all is quiet. In the dim light, the three sleeping forms of two Officers and an N.C.O., the floor completely covered by protruding feet, blankets, and greatcoats. The Signaller at his post.

32

33

7.

34

24

32: 'Letter for Home'   Mareth Line front, 7th March 1943.

Rommel attacks at dawn! On the crest, the usual morning patrol take their positions. Suddenly, towards the Mareth Line, the enemy guns open fire! The barrage rises to a crescendo! The knowledge that an attack is being made steels the senses. As light of day becomes clearer, the patrol creeps slowly, one by one, from the trenches and crawls over the ridge. Commands are shouted.... the gunners at their post.... the Battery awaits orders.

The steady waiting.... pulses quicken.... and then 'Take Post'. Orders are passed down.... the electrifying Command - 'Fire'. As though sprung with a thousand springs, the 25-pounders go into action. Throughout the day no slackening. The range gets shorter.... anxious moments.... only 900 yards.... tanks on the left.... rear Observation Post established.... cold and wet night.... the watch for encirclement.... and then the welcome dawn! The enemy repulsed, the guns are silent! The 'Tommy' rests and eats. Finale - the letter for home - written with a thankful heart! The line stands firm!

33: 'Signaller in the Command Post, 3.30am'   Mareth Line front, 10th March 1943.

Excitement throughout the day. Shells fall uncomfortably close. The deep Wadi accentuates the explosion. Sound and flash, deeper, brighter! Earth, stone, and shrapnel everywhere. A terrific explosion to our right.... a high spiral column of smoke from an ammunition truck.... a direct hit!

The 'recce' party moves out.... due to return late evening. Night falls.... no news. The Command Post filled with anxious O.C. and officers. The Signaller strains his ears.... clasped to his head, the phones. Hands held lightly over the head-frame, shutting out outside sound. Microphone held to mouth. Deliberate calling signals.... a pause.... and no answer. Hours pass. Suddenly his body is taut.... a signal at last.... Faint.... they are in contact! The O.C.'s command to return.... the transmission clear and concise.... the deliberate up-movement of the hand-switch.... 'They've got it'. Speech is more distinct. The party is lying low.... 'Germans not far away.... waiting till morning.... off'. Anxiety is now past. The Signaller hands his set to the next on duty. The lamp shadows flicker across sleeping forms. All is quiet!

34: 'Telephone exchange'   Mareth Line front, 10th March 1943.

Large rocks form the bed of the Wadi and, between two large boulders, with a sandbagged entrance, is the little "Exchange". Here is the nerve-centre of battery communications with the R.H.Q. The loss or destruction of its mechanism could isolate the whole position. Unusually well concealed and protected, its small precincts are the envy of outside mortals! Extremely heavy shelling of the position sends men clambering for safety. Despite the tight press of bodies the operator still calmly handles the switchboard with cool nerves and a cool head. A shell drops so close by that the little dugout trembles. A loose sandbag breaks so the sanded earth trickles from torn canvas. The few men gaze strangely around - the agonised wait for the next missile. It explodes a little further away, so the men breathe easier. Someone laughs and the spell is broken. Chatter and relaxation follow. Through it all the Signaller works with no show of fear. The communications are intact.

35

36

7

35: 'Anti-aircraft gun site' Mareth Line front, 11th March 1943.

The raiders come out of the sun.... the ack-ack gunners are at their stations. Swinging the long muzzle towards the enemy planes, they load and re-load. The loud staccato of shell explosions.... the falling bombs.... a sense of frailty.... the raiders pass. They have missed the guns, thank God!

A short lull, then high in the blue sky a returning Squadron of enemy planes. All around their fascinating shapes - flak. The barrage becomes more intense. Suddenly a plane appears out of control.... the swaying fuselage flies straight into its companion. The momentary interlocking of planes.... tense faces on the ground break into smiles.... cheers, as parts of aircraft fall as leaves in a storm. A small black object races to earth.... the pilot, his parachute fails! One is lucky - his parachute opens. A pleasing picture on a scarred background.... the whiteness of his 'chute against the blue sky. Slowly the long muzzle of the gun is lowered. Sweating men dismount. The ordeal is over! Good work 'ack-ack'!

36: 'The battery cookhouse' Mareth Line front, 12th March 1943.

Under incessant shell-fire from Rommel's guns, the diligent cooks prepare the meals of the day. The night before, rations would be taken from the Quartermaster's truck.... tinned potatoes, carrots, fruit, and the most famous dish 'out here' - M & V.

The morning breakfast.... Scotsmen's relish - porridge with salt.... and the Englishman's banter - for his choice, a little sugar! Meal times were not free from danger. A shell would fall a little way up the Wadi. Halfway across with full mess tin and mug of tea.... crouching down.... apprehensive lest another should come over.... a low half-run to gain the shelter of a bank of earth. Muttered oaths.... now half-spilled tea and scattered food.... The 'reward' of a hectic interruption! The cooks ladle out. The 'Tommies' make their way. Meal over, a chat, then the smoking of a 'V' cigarette.

37: 'A Forward Patrol Post' Mareth Line front, March 1943.

The day draws to a close. The fast receding light sees the Forward Patrol of the gun position move out. An Officer leads, his N.C.O. and men disappear over the ridge. Darkness now falls. Stars begin to twinkle in the sky.... no moon.... the air crisp and cold.... men wrapped in mufflers and greatcoats.... gloves over mittens.

Half-way maintenance post reached.... the turn of duty allotted. The next small group walk quietly to the advance post. In the black distance, the Mareth Line. Forward patrols begin their night work. The drone of aircraft - ours! The settling into a more comfortable position in the dugout.... eyes pierce the gloom.... senses alert. In the distance a flash.... another, and yet another. The low rumbles of falling bombs reach our ears. A glow flares quickly into a bright yellow-red, and a myriad tiny stars burst in the sky. Bombs explode on the target.... the glow settles.... an ammunition dump has gone! The night gets colder. To keep alert is an effort. Relief comes.

38

39

38: 'Trig' point and native quarters' — Mareth Line front, 14th March 1943.

Rain falls - a refreshing shower - but unfortunately spoils the preparations for drawing. The cab of a 'four-wheeled drive' gun tractor, commonly known as a 'Quad', proves adequate protection from the rain. On completion of the drawing, a closer inspection of the rude huts surprises one. Rough mattress-like beds, made from branches and straw, form the main comfort of the inmates. In the adjoining hut a rough stall for the ass. Fleas abound.... a hasty retreat!

The day draws to a close. After the evening meal, groups of men around bivouacs, chatting of home, and the ever-absorbing topic of sport. Away to the right, a shell falls near the track.... the startled faces.... it is quite unexpected. Bodies are now tense. Suddenly the whine of a shell.... and crunch.... the missile explodes to our rear! Figures disappear.... a few adventurous 'Tommies' sit on the edge of trenches, ready to dive for cover. No more shells.... and the light of day fades quickly.... it is night!

39: 'Flash-spotting tower' — Mareth Line front, 15th March 1943.

The freshness of the morning proved a beneficial aid to health, the morning dew leaving the bivouacs limp till the early sun's rays would tighten ropes and canvas. Breakfast casually eaten 'neath the spreading leaves of an olive tree. The wagon lines dispersed among the olive groves, the trucks backed close to the trunks. Spreading branches cover the tell-tale shapes and shadows.

The peculiar tower across the distant cornfield, known as a 'flash-spotting tower', dominates the landscape. Closer scrutiny shows the tiny figure of a man climbing the girder-work and pacing the platform at the top. The figure stops.... observes the enemy's gun flashes.... information is gleaned and passed on. Below on the ground the breeze gently sways the tops of the corn stalks. The silent, deserted native huts, too dirty and filthy for close inspection, spoil the morning scene.

40

40: 'Tommy cleans his rifle' — Mareth Line front, 16th March 1943.

The brilliant sun shines in the blue sky. Deep shadows fall from the over-hanging olive trees. The cool breeze brings refreshing relief from the warm rays of the sun. The day is given to general maintenance. The Signallers re-charge batteries, tinker with wireless and telephone sets. Drivers go through their daily task. Engine hoods are taken off.... figures sprawl beneath shadowed chassis.

A figure sits beneath a large tree, its branches almost envelop the vehicle behind him. The rifle - a soldier's best friend - is in his hand, bolt and magazine at his side. The 'pull-through' to clean the bore hangs from a branch. With great care and pride, the ritual of daily cleaning has become a habit. The monotony of desert life is broken - the 'Tommy' always has something to do!

[Four days later, on the 20th, there is something in the air. Rommel failed to throw us back - is it now our turn? Then word comes through and everyone gets his orders. Equipment is made ready. The Quartermaster's area is agog with activity. The air is alive with Allied aircraft as they go over in eighteens. We are resting on the eve of battle!]

41

42

41: 'In a Tunisian palm grove'   After Mareth, 1st April 1943.

The Mareth Battle is past! General Montgomery's famous left-hook has forced the enemy to retreat! Our first view of a large oasis! Between two large concrete pillboxes, and towards the palm grove ahead, vehicles and guns move forward. Signs of habitation. Natives appear, of a better appearance than those already encountered.

Camouflage completed, the palm fronds, laid on the vehicles, perfect the illusion! Deeper in the grove are native quarters, with neatly tilled soil - which proves a pleasant surprise! A native shows us where we can get a drink. He makes his way to a tall frond-less palm, and proceeds to climb. Reaching the top he dips a small jar into the hollow trunk. We watch his descent. He hands over the drink. A doubtful sipping.... it's sweetness is pleasing to the taste! Later exploration finds in a charred clearing the black remains of a plane, the engine buried-deep in the ground. Broken and torn trees form a ring of forlorn sentinels!

42: 'Pol Lapeyz Barracks'   Sfax, 18th April 1943.

April 6th saw the fierce battle of Wadi Akarit, and the undying glory of a Battalion of the Argyll and Sutherland Highlanders. They were led by Col. Lome Campbell who, in this engagement, won the Victoria Cross.

A short respite at Sfax.... a much needed rest.... the town, unfortunately, so battle-scarred that the troops were robbed of pleasant shopping tours. Here the famous Balmoral Concert Party made their Headquarters in the French cavalry barracks. The recent occupation of enemy troops was in evidence. Destroyed, wheel-less cars blocked the narrow roadways and paths. Only the spacious courtyard provided adequate space. However, the adaptability of the Army soon became evident. Large garages and stables formed excellent workshops, the fitters already at work repairing trucks and Bren-carriers. In another part of the barracks, the kilted pipers preparing for a ceremonial parade. Last, but not least, good sleeping quarters!

43

43: 'Blown up oil barge'   Near Sousse, 7th May 1943.

Rest periods from camp life formed one of the main relaxations between battles. A spot near the sea was preferable, for bathing was of paramount importance to health. Parties of men would pitch their bivouacs or mosquito nets in shady bowers. Natives were friendly, bringing produce from the fields. Greed for eggs knew no bounds.... this luxury no longer denied.

The long sandy beach glistening white against the blue of the sea. A bright morning.... a long walk through fields and olive groves.... a wall enclosed native quarters. Women scampered away at our approach, frightened children keeping behind thick walls. We passed by, they came out. On the beach.... a dark object ahead. Investigation.... a burnt-out barge, obviously scuttled, its nose facing deserted, scarred buildings. In the distance, the port of Sousse. Beyond lay the last bastion of the Germans, and Cape Carbon.

44

45

32